CONTENTS

EDITOR'S PREFACE

The books in the *Changing Geography* series seek to alert students in schools and colleges to current developments in university geography. It also aims to close the gap between school and university geography. This is not a knee-jerk response – that school and college geography should be necessarily a watered down version of higher education approaches – but a deeper recognition that students in post-16 education should be exposed to the ideas currently being taught and researched in universities. Many such ideas are of interest to young people and relevant to their lives (and school examinations).

The series introduces post-16 students to concepts and ideas that tend to be excluded from conventional school texts. Written in language which is readily accessible, illustrated with contemporary case studies, including numerous suggestions for discussion, projects and fieldwork, and lavishly illustrated, the books in this series push post-16 geography into the realm of modern geographical thinking.

In this book the geography of sport is explored at a variety of geographical scales and in a wide range of contexts. Though geographers have traditionally been interested in 'leisure', relatively little has been done to apply geographical ideas to the study of the kinds of activities that fill up the sports pages of our newspapers. Students will look in vain in most geography books for ideas on the varied geographies of, for example, athletics, football and tennis. *Sportscapes* seeks to resolve the paradox that what many students find interesting is denied to them in school geography courses. It shows how in a variety of situations, a number of geographical principles can be applied to inform our view of sport and its impact on environment and society.

Sportscapes will also be of use to students following courses in Sociology, Sports studies and Leisure and recreation.

John Bale
August 2000

600075541X

University of Hertfordshire

College Lane, Hatfield, Herts. AL10 9AB

Learning and Information Services

For renewal of Standard and One Week Loans,
please visit the web site **http://www.voyager.herts.ac.uk**

This item must be returned or the loan renewed by the due date.
The University reserves the right to recall items from loan at any time.
A fine will be charged for the late return of items.

NG
RAPHY

TOR: JOHN BALE

scapes

BALE

Geographical
Association

ACKNOWLEDGEMENTS

I am grateful to Bob Jones for helpful comments on a draft of this book. I also acknowledge Edexcel for permission to reproduce the material on pages 24-27. I take full responsibility for the contents of what follows.

The Geographical Association would like to thank the following individuals and organisations for permission to reproduce material:

- Graham Watson for the images of cyclists used on the front cover and page 12.
- The Olympic Co-ordination Authority for Figure 4, page 11 and the front cover image of Stadium Australia.
- The Bank of England for Figure 13, page 33.
- Professional Footballers' Association for Figure 14 on page 34.

AUTHOR: John Bale is Professor of Sports Geography at Keele University, Staffordshire.

ISBN 1 899085 86 6
First published 2000
Impression number 10 9 8 7 6 5 4 3 2 1
Year 2003 2002 2001

Published by the Geographical Association, 160 Solly Street, Sheffield S1 4BF. The Geographical Association is a registered charity: no 313129.

The Publications Officer of the GA would be happy to hear from other potential authors who have ideas for geography books. You may contact the Officer via the GA at the address above.

Edited by Rose Pipes
Designed by ATG Design, Catalyst Creative Imaging, Leeds
Printed and bound in Hong Kong by Colorcraft Ltd.

INTRODUCTION

Whether we like it or not, it would be difficult to deny that sport is an important aspect of modern life. Indeed, in England and Wales we are obliged to participate in it, as part of the National Curriculum for Physical Education. Massive time is devoted to sport on television, and events like the Cup Final, Wimbledon, Test Matches, the Boat Race, the Derby and the London Marathon are part of the national heritage. Sport is generally thought of as a 'good thing'; those who dislike it are seen as 'spoil-sports'. But what has it got to do with geography? Well, apart from the fact that all sports events possess *sites* and *locations*, geographical interest has recently been shown in, for example, the *places* (e.g. stadiums) where sports are performed, the *relocation* of sports teams (notably in football), the *ecological* effects of sports (such as golf and skiing), the international *migration* of sports talent, the *globalisation* of the sports goods industry, and the *sustainability* of the Olympic Games. Sport is not without controversy; it is not as 'innocent' as it sometimes seems. In this book I will:

- show how geography is central to an understanding of modern sport;
- illustrate how sports exemplify locational and ecological problems, often involving conflict and politics;
- suggest that sport and its geographies involve ethical and even spiritual dimensions;
- reveal how, in sport, global pressures are often revealed at the local scale;
- show how a geography of sport can utilise ideas and skills found widely in other areas of geographical study.

For convenience, I have used a scale-based approach in assembling the book's ideas (though in reality all geographical scales are intimately related). I have also introduced a variety of geographical approaches to the study of sports, which reflect both traditional and recent developments in geography. For example, in some places, I have suggested and illustrated numerical methods of analysing geographical differences. In other places I have shown how a literary analysis of texts can reveal and suggest hidden meanings that might lurk in the representations of sports. This engagement with written and visual texts (and, indeed, the viewing of the landscapes of, say, the cricket ground or the running track as 'texts' to be excavated) reflects more recent thinking in human geography.

CHAPTER 1

DEFINING SPORT AND ITS GEOGRAPHIES

'Sport' is one of those words that is difficult to define. It seems to be used to define almost any physical activity ranging from darts to dancing, from chess to cricket, from fishing to football. One is tempted to think that because the word 'sport' can be applied to so many things, it has no meaning at all. It is such a slippery term that it begs to be 'made real', to be 'thingified'. Many people would regard 'running' as a sport. But if we stop to think about it, running could take several forms. Children running freely in a field or on a beach could be said to be frolicking for fun. This could be called 'play sport'. Playing, in its purest form, cannot be forced on people; it is spontaneous, and it is difficult to conceive of being 'made to play'. The objective of play-sport is to have fun, to indulge the senses, to let the body be free. Consider now a second type of running that you might undertake for another reason: that is, to keep fit and healthy. This might be as part of a physical education class, going out jogging, or as running on a machine in a fitness studio. Here, the objective is not so much to have fun but to keep fit. Its aim, I suggest, is that of welfare – helping to make the body healthy and fit (for the world of work, some observers would add). I will call this 'welfare sport'. The athletes who take part in the Olympic 100m final could illustrate a third form of running. These athletes are hardly 'playing', nor (arguably) are they keeping fit. They are engaged in the deadly serious business of what can be called 'achievement sport'.

Another difference between each of these kinds of running is that they take place in a different environment or place: the 100m final cannot be held on a beach or in a field, or in a gymnasium or an aerobics studio; it requires a specified space. But we do not *need* an Olympic stadium in which to have fun. The aim of play sport is fun and frolic; that of achievement sport is a victory or a record. Clearly, the motives of those who take part in each of these kinds of sports are different – and so are their geographies.

For the most part, it is achievement sport that I will be dealing with in this book. This form of sport has traditionally been much more gendered than play or welfare sports. It was men who, in the mid- to late-nineteenth century, drew up the rules and regulations of most achievement sports. Women were discouraged, even banned, from taking part in many sports and opposition to mixed-gender sport remains to the present day. Achievement sport refers to the kinds of sports that we read about (mainly) on the sports pages of our newspapers. However, because play sport and welfare sport may, sometimes, come close to the achievement model (when they are taken more seriously or competitively for example), I will not totally disregard them.

The above preamble is illustrated in Figure 1, which shows three 'models' of 'sport', drawing on the ideas of the sports historian Henning Eichberg (1998). Each of the models shown in the diagram is an 'ideal type' – that is, a generalisation or a hypothetical norm against which the complexity of the real world can be better appreciated. Figure 1 suggests that according to different underlying sports ideologies activity may be:

(a) focused on increasing the output of records and victories (the pyramid model),
(b) aiming to reproduce a fit population, or
(c) simply having fun.

Figure 1: Three forms of sport space. Source: Bale, 1983.

Ideology is generally thought of in one of two ways:

1. a set of ideas that provide a collective consciousness or a generalised system of ideas, and
2. a consciousness that is in some ways 'false' and which fails to grasp the real conditions of human life, i.e. a distorted system of ideas.

The overall model can be made more 'realistic' if arrows are drawn between the three forms of body culture to show that elements of one may influence any one of the others. So a play-like element may enter achievement sport while welfare values may enter the play-like model.

The arrows also suggest that one type of sport may contest another, indicating that there may be geographical differences in the kinds of sports in which people participate. Some countries may seek to exclude the idea of élite or achievement sport, as was the case in Maoist China, where 'trophyism' was regarded as too individualistic. Likewise, in schools, education polices may shift between putting more or less emphasis on team games, depending on the philosophies or ideologies of those who prescribe the curriculum. My key point is that different geographies (and different human bodies) accompany each of the types of sport shown in Figure 1, and different kinds of spaces are assigned to each form of sport. If we did not adopt the achievement sport ideology, many of the buildings and landscapes, sights and sites, that we take for granted (stadiums, running tracks, rectangular swimming pools) would simply not exist. The sport landscape can therefore be said to be ideological.

Sport as geography

Sport could be regarded as a kind of applied geography. Sports, argued the geographer Philip Wagner (1981), are about struggles over space and the conquest of territory. Wagner drew attention to the strongly geographical (that is spatial) nature of sports. We often hear football commentators talking about players 'making space'. Sports sites are geometrically and mathematically ordered spaces defined by boundaries and segments – the 20.12m (22 yards) of the 'wicket' in cricket; the 23.77m (78 feet) of the tennis court, the 11m (12 yards) from the goal line to the penalty spot in football. Additionally,

sports have been recorded statistically, in some cases for over a century, in books like *Rothman's Football Yearbook* and *Wisden's Cricketers' Almanac* (each of which is a wonderful resource for geographical research). The accurate measurements of sport's spaces are part of the rules of sports. They place great stress on the geographical limits within which sport can take place. 'Space' is therefore a central concept in both geography and sports. And all the quantification in sports seems to make them eminently 'scientific'.

Achievement sports are also identified strongly with another basic geographical concept, that of 'place'. Serious sports can be said to be 'representational'. This means that they symbolically represent places. These places may be schools, universities, cities, counties or nations. Almost all élite sports teams are named after places. In the case of individual sports, players are also often felt to be representing the places (nations) that they come from. Few activities (except, perhaps, war) can represent places in the way sports do. So, space and place are central concepts in both geography and sports.

In Chapters 2 to 5 I work from the local to the global. Chapter 2 looks at sites and sights at the level of the sports place – the body, the arena and course. Chapter 3 moves to the city scale, looking at the relationship between sport and the city and Chapter 4 investigates sport at the national scale, while Chapter 5 examines sports at international and global scales. While this approach appears convenient (and that is the main reason for choosing it), it can also be misleading. It suggests that the scales are in some way separate from each other, which is not the case. The stadium, for example, draws on the city and region for the crowds that fill it (pages 28-9). It is also connected in various ways to the global 'reality' of sports – the rules administered by global federations (e.g. the Fédération Internationale de Football Association, the International Amateur Athletics Federation) (pages 36-7), the international movement of 'sports labour' and the global corporations that manufacture sports goods (pages 38-9). Therefore, it is not really possible to understand what is going on in the stadium by looking at the stadium alone.

CHAPTER 2

SPORTS: BODIES, SITES AND STADIUMS

For many people, the most familiar features of sports are the places where they are 'played' and watched. Wimbledon, Wembley, Twickenham, Henley, Brands Hatch, Epsom and St Andrews are places that are known (by name, at least) to many people who have not the slightest interest in the sports that take place there. These places are the sites and sights of sports. This chapter shows how these places are not simply buildings or facilities. They are ambiguous features of a city's (or a region's) geography, subject to different 'ways of seeing'.

Superficially, the sites of sports vary considerably. However, some important generalities about sports places tell us something about the character of achievement sport. For a start, many sports sites are highly prescribed:

- a football pitch can only be of a certain size, containing maximum and minimum spatial limits;
- all tennis courts must be the same size;
- for a world record to be acceptable in athletics, it must be made on a track of a prescribed size.

It might be more fun to watch a tennis match with one half of the court a different size from the other, and with each court having its own idiosyncratic markings, but it would simply not be consistent with sport's ideology. As Wagner (1981) observed, the landscape of sport is made up of very 'closely defined *conventionalised* places'. There is little place for the unconventional in serious sports. In this chapter I want to show how the sites of sport have become increasingly conventional and serious – in response to the achievement ideology – over time.

Before they came to be regarded as 'sports', a number of sport-like activities had no standardised geographical limits and players and spectators were virtually indistinguishable from each other (Figure 2, stage 1). Such activities could be described as pre-modern 'folk-games'. These were rough and tumble contests with very loose rules and did not occupy special sites. Legacies of these traditions remain in 'folk' forms today, as in the Shrove Tuesday football at

Ashbourne in Derbyshire and the Eton Wall game (Figure 3). In some parts of the world, these kinds of folk-games are being revived. They fit the fun model of sport better than the achievement model.

Gradually, as rules evolved (mainly from the mid-nineteenth century onwards), sites became characterised by the separation of players from spectators. It may not be surprising that this 'enclosure' more or less coincided with the enclosure of common land. Clearly marked boundaries – usually a white line marking the spatial limits of the activity – communicated the imposition of territoriality on the sports environment. Spectators were allowed

STAGES	ENVIRONMENT
1	PERMEABLE BOUNDARIES WEAK RULES OF EXCLUSION No spatial limits; uneven terrain; spatial interaction between 'players' and 'spectators'; diversified land use.
2	ENCLOSURE Limits of pitch defined; players segregated from spectators.
3	PARTITIONING Embankments, terraces, grandstands; payment for entry; segregation of spectators by social class; start of segregation within crowd; specialised land use
4	SURVEILLANCE Enclosed ground; synthetic pitch and concrete bowl; TV replay screen; total segregation within crowd; panopticism; diversified land use. RULES OF EXCLUSION STRONG, IMPERMEABLE BOUNDARIES

Figure 2: A four-stage model of the stadium. Arrows show movement of 'players' (red arrows) and spectators (green arrows).

Figure 3: The Eton Wall game. Image: Mary Evans Picture Library.

considerable freedom within the stadium to sit where they liked and to move around – but it had to be beyond the boundary. They were excluded from the field of 'play' (Figure 2, stage 2). As sport became more popular for spectators, admission charges could be made and sports became commodities. Superior accommodation (a covered stand, for example) was provided for those who could afford it (Figure 2, stage 3). For much of the twentieth century, most achievement sport was practised in specialised sports spaces. Most could not be used for anything but the one or two sports for which they were designed. Many, like football grounds, could not even be used for recreational versions of the sport for which they were constructed. They were often described as football or cricket grounds, rather than sports stadiums. In football, during the 1970s, stadiums increasingly became further segmented so that home and away supporters were physically separated from each other. Such segregation sought to increase order in the stadium during a period when football hooliganism was increasing.

For many sports there has also been a growing tendency over the last century towards 'sameness'. This means that one swimming pool, football pitch, tennis court, running track, basketball court, ice hockey rink, etc., looks more or less the same as any other. As noted on page 9, they often have to be the same to satisfy the rules of the sport. Of course, in the design of stadium or arena facilities beyond the area on which the action takes place, architects are allowed to impose their whims. However, there has, from time to time, been a tendency to make these also look very much alike, so one place becomes much the same as any other. Architects refer to 'concrete saucers' or 'bunker architecture' to describe such facilities.

In addition to this growing confinement and sameness, a further tendency has been for sports sites to become increasingly synthetic. The natural environment as a site for sport has been replaced by an artificial one, on which increasingly artificial bodies perform (see Information Box 1, page 12). Many new facilities are more ambiguous and less easily identified with a particular sport or activity. Such diversification has, in large part, arisen from the need to increase revenue, with facilities being used more intensively than the older, single-purpose 'grounds'. Their multi-functional character has led them to be called 'post-modern' in design. For example, swimming pools have been supplemented or replaced by 'water worlds' where, instead of or as well as, swimming individually in a lane (Figure 4a), it is possible to slide and splash in a more social and convivial environment (Figure 4b). Likewise, anyone approaching the SkyDome Stadium (Figure 5) in Toronto, Canada could easily mistake it for a hotel, a conference centre or a series of restaurants. It is actually all of these things. In such facilities the lines between leisure, sport and entertainment become so blurred that they are neither one thing nor the other.

You will have probably recognised that while spatial regulation is obvious in the case of, say, the football stadium, it might seem to be missing in other sports sites. Take, for example, golf courses, which

---

■ **Activity Box 1: Fieldwork investigation**

Visit some local sports stadiums and centres and consider:

1. What kinds of non-sporting activities (e.g. museum, gift shops, banqueting facilities) take place in them?
2. Establish in what ways they have become multi-purpose facilities that encourage spending.
3. Try to discover the extent to which they can be regarded as a 'community' resource.

Figure 4: Part of the Sydney Olympic complex,
Australia: (a) the Olympic pool, and (b) Water World.
Photos: Olympic Co-ordination Authority and John Bale.

Loneliness of the Long Distance Runner (Sillitoe, 1961). Smith defies the codes of sport by stopping just before the finishing line and allowing a runner from the private school (against whom his prison team is competing) to win. By winning the race Smith would have been conforming to the expectations of 'the system'; by stepping outside the sport's space he became a 'spoil-sport'.

Marxist observers such as Jean-Marie Brohm (1978) and Bero Rigauer (1981) have argued that achievement sport is a form of work or a 'prison of

seem to differ from each other in some way, and which also appear (misleadingly) to be more 'natural'. The same might be said of orienteering or cross-country running courses. However, in each case, the activities take place in finite spaces. Golf, orienteering events and cross-country running have well-defined starting and finishing points. If participants want to stop before the finishing line or the eighteenth hole, they are taking themselves out of sport. Such actions could be read as a kind of resistance, reminiscent of the fictional juvenile delinquent, Colin Smith, in The

Figure 5: The approach to the SkyDome, Toronto. Photo: John Bale.

measured time' (geographers might say a 'prison of measured space'). The extent to which participants (I can't really call them 'players' when they are 'working' at sports) and spectators are 'imprisoned' within their own bodies and within stadiums is discussed next.

Confining the body

The notion of the body enclosed in a confined space seems to be the antithesis of the free body associated with play. However, sports-workers are not programmed machines, as the antics of some 'clown-like' individuals demonstrate. Many spectators experience the thrill of success or the despair of defeat in their own bodies, sometimes engaging more with other spectators or players than is sanctioned by society. Shouting and singing can transcend the line separating the spectators from the players. Indeed, such a presence may be able to influence the result of a game. The boundary between the fans and the players – the clear line separating the players/workers from the spectators – is more permeable than it appears at first sight. In some 'trash sports', like professional wrestling, a permeable boundary between 'players' and 'spectators' is essential for the success of the performance.

Another way of looking at the 'sportised' body being confined is by looking at its relationship to machinery of various kinds. The mechanisation of the body goes back to the early days of 'machine sport',

notably cycling, which made the body move faster. In cycling, motor sports and water sports the body and the machine become one. Each is dependent on the other.

If drugs and medicaments are added to the body, to make it move faster (or 'better'), the sport-body can be seen as de-sexualised (bodybuilding and drug taking, for example, can blur the distinction between 'male' and 'female') – a 'cyborg' body (see Information Box 1).

Ways of seeing the stadium

There are several ways of 'reading' the stadium, three of which – the prison, the garden and the cathedral – are conceptualised below. The use of these three metaphors reveals sports places as ambiguous sites, landscapes whose 'meaning' can be read and contested in much the same way as one could read different things into the text of a book or film.

'The prison'

First, the metaphor of 'the prison' can be applied to spectators (as well as athletes, as described above). Consider the following statement:

> **'This enclosed, segmented space, observed at every point, in which individuals are inserted in a fixed place in which the slightest movements are supervised, in which all events are recorded.'**

Information Box 1: The cyborg body

'The natural body becomes an object superfluous to the operation of a post-modern sports system. The natural body is covered with aerodynamically-designed clothes; shaved for speed; locked into ankle, knee, arm, and neck braces; invaded by diuretics, growth hormones, high-calorie food, vitamins, carbohydrates, "pure blood" and multiple drugs; divided into parts to be separately trained and shaped by computerized machines; and divided into pieces that are sometimes thrown away and replaced by artificial versions (e.g. Teflon articulations). The natural body disappears. In modern times, the image was modelled after the human body. In post-modernity, the reverse is true: the human body is modelled after the image.'

Source: Rail, 1998, pp. 150-1.

Photo: Graham Watson.

This could be a description of the all-seater stadium where, it could be said, people sit passively in numbered seats watching the sporting spectacle unwind before their eyes. Their 'slightest movement' can be recorded by the ever-present video camera. However, the quote comes from *Discipline and Punish: The history of the prison* by the French cultural theorist, Michel Foucault (1979, p. 197). Through this lens, the stadium is seen as a container of 'docile' bodies subject to continuous surveillance. The players have their place – and their places (i.e. positions) – on the field of play (or work) and the spectators have theirs in the stands. This pessimistic perspective, in which everyone knows their place, is commonly presented as one view of late-modern sport, part of a society of the spectacle in which people pay to have themselves physically (and mentally/emotionally?) controlled (see Information Box 2).

'The garden'

The second metaphor for a stadium is that of the garden or the park. These carry connotations of playfulness, places of freedom, islands of greenery in the asphalt and concrete of the city, away from the restriction of indoors. Grass, trees and plants resonate with nature. Many stadiums and arenas are *called*

Information Box 2: A brave new (sports) world?

What follows is the content of an e-mail sent to the author on 9 March 2000, a few months before the 'Euro 2000' football championship.

'According to an article in the Spanish newspaper *El País*, the organisers of the Euro 2000 football tournament are placing all kinds of control on the acquisition of tickets and then on the behaviour that will be permitted within the stadium. First of all, people who purchase tickets must provide all sorts of personal data – name, address, identity card number, etc. This data can be given to police and other government agencies, and be presented to third parties for commercial purposes. Second, if you purchase a ticket for someone else you will also be responsible for his/her behaviour and subject to being fined by the "Euro 2000 Foundation" if he or she doesn't behave. Finally, once inside the stadium the fan is subject to the following restrictions: no arms, drugs or drink, no promotional or commercial material, e.g. symbols, posters, insignias. The wearing of costumes and expressing "nationalist or political ideas" is prohibited and security forces in the stadium will determine the correct or incorrect behaviour. The justification for all this is to ensure that people don't buy blocks of tickets for the purpose of selling them and because of supposed hooliganism.

I found the article funny and scary. Funny, because it seems a bit over the top – I am somehow imagining that it can't really be true, that it is just some group of over-zealous Euro Cup organisers. Scary, because it is obviously "fascist", or quasi-fascist at least in its intent. You could also assume that this is a kind of ideal state for the organisers and it will not have anything to do with the reality of the sale of tickets or the behaviour inside the stadiums. It raises the question what is the point of the live audience to the organisers? From this article you could assume that the organisers would prefer there to be no live audience, or rather one that behaves as if at a tennis match.'

Source: Jed Rosenstein, e-mail communication, 9 March 2000.

Activity Box 2: Confining sports

The following questions can form the focus of a whole-class discussion on the role of professional sports people and spectators in sport.

1. In what ways could watching professional sports be regarded as similar to being in a prison?
2. Do you think that there is any place for free expression or 'play' in modern professional sport within the confines of white lines?
3. What do you think the author of the e-mail in Information Box 2 means by 'fascist' in this context?
4. In what ways do spectators at tennis matches behave differently from football spectators?
5. How might sports fans promote 'political ideas'?

Photo: Dave Clark/Swift Picture Library.

parks or gardens, for example, Sophia Gardens, Cardiff (home of Glamorgan Cricket Club) or Goodison Park (home of Everton Football Club). But these so-called parks and gardens are landscapes devoted to specialised economic activities. They include concrete buildings and carefully manicured and scientifically bred turf. Their names do not denote what they really are; yet, like a park or garden, the sports stadium continues to combine horticulture and architecture (many are not yet totally synthetic).

The most garden- or park-like landscape of sport is arguably the golf course. Like the domestic garden, the golf course is nurtured, cut, maintained and sculptured. Nature is totally dominated yet still loved and tended. Originally played on the coastal links of Scotland, golf has today colonised deserts and forests. The 'natural' landscapes on which the early courses were located have replicated on inland courses, a process that involves huge expense and effort. American geographer Robert Adams has described how the modern golf course:

'often begins with moving hundreds of thousands of cubic yards of material to re-contour the terrain in order to accommodate the construction of trees, fairways and greens to exact prescriptions. Top soil, often with additives, is then replaced and seeded with special, non-native strains of grass. The grass is nurtured by the application of huge quantities of fertilisers, herbicides, fungicides and pesticides and the construction of elaborate irrigation systems. Mowing is accomplished with sophisticated machinery so that the height of the grass is exactingly controlled. Fairways, and particularly greens, are repeatedly aerated and top dressed. The results are uniform, lush, soft, velvety-smooth carpets of grass' (Adams, 1995, pp. 244-5)

The time and motion expert F.W. Taylor influenced early golf course design in the USA. An enthusiastic golfer, he spent the final years of his life experimenting with the growing of grass. Virginia Scott Jenkins (1994) reports how Taylor sought to standardise putting greens, with grass being made in a similar way to a product in a factory. He saw the golf course as a manufactured and predictable object.

If the greens of golf courses are what have been called 'prototypical domestic lawns', where are the houses that front on to these lawns? The garden metaphor is reinforced when we realise that many golf courses, in the UK and the USA, are today being constructed with houses integral to them – what are basically golf-oriented communities. Such 'fairway housing' (Figure 6) results from the fact that landowners or developers may have to wait up to seven years for a return on their investment and therefore need some kind of ancillary development to 'carry the golf course'. Such developments reflect the way that sports represent a development opportunity for several other land-uses. In addition to housing, ancillary developments might include other leisure facilities or a hotel. Where facilities such as children's playgrounds and swimming pools are added, the golf course becomes part of a broader leisure complex. Bradley Klein (1999) suggests that golf courses have come to look less like local land than the image propagated by big business. Rural land, which was once a focus for the *production* of crops and animals, becomes a site for the *consumption* of sport.

Activity Box 3: Sports places as gardens

1. Discuss the extent to which the 'garden' metaphor adequately describes the modern sports space.
2. Do you feel that human beings dominate nature when, for example, they lovingly tend a grass tennis court?
3. If sports places are 'gardens', is the sport participant a 'pet'? Consider the extent to which the sport coach treats his or her athlete as a 'pet'. (In this context you might like to read: Tuan, 1984.)

Figure 6: A golf-oriented community under construction near Crewe, Cheshire. Here, the construction of the golf course is being supplemented by a residential development. Photo: John Bale.

'The cathedral'

The third metaphor that might be used to describe the stadium is that of the cathedral – a site of holiness. Like cathedrals, the stadium contains rituals; like the

cathedral the stadium is a much-loved place. Many stadiums generate what the geographer Yi-Fu Tuan (1974) termed 'topophilia' – a love of place. People develop a strong sense of place for such buildings. For them it is their 'home' ground. The idea of topophilia helps explain the strong attachment many people have for 'their' ground. Some stadiums come to achieve almost religious significance as a result of the overwhelming experiences people have within them. Consider the following quote from a Manchester City Football Club fan:

> 'I have been a supporter since my parents first took me when I was around two years old ... my interest has revolved more around the stadium than the team. Of course, I support the team, but to me the club is Maine Road ... Managers, players, directors and even supporters come and go but the stadium never disappears.'

Religious metaphors and language are often used to describe sports stadiums, as in *Green Cathedrals* – a book about American baseball stadiums (Lowry, 1983). There are also the quasi-religious rituals performed before the game by players and coaches – and fans. Consider the language and imagery in the following quote from a fan, describing the former 'home' (another powerful metaphor) of Chester City Football Club:

> 'Sealand Road is more than a football ground, it's a way of life ... to thousands of people alive and dead whose life has revolved around a match at the stadium. It's more than bricks and mortar; it's almost something spiritual.'

If sacred places are those of 'overpowering significance' (as Tuan (1980) would suggest) then it is difficult to deny that places of sports are sacred. A love of place is stimulated by senses such as sight, sound

Cartoon: Dave Howarth

Activity Box 4: A sports sense of place

Consider the ways in which a 'sense of place' may exist in particular sports places in your locality.

1. Do you think 'a sense of place' is reduced in newer, multi-purpose sports facilities?
2. Do you think sports places are becoming 'McDonalised'?
3. What contributes to 'a sense of place' in a sports location known to you?
4. How, in sports, might you have a negative 'sense of place' ('topophobia')?

Discuss these issues as a class.

---

and smells that record events of great significance to the person concerned. In the case of a sports stadium, such events contribute to geographical memory and urban identity. Inside the sports arena there is a huge range of visual experiences to be consumed; indeed, the sports spectacle is about seeing. An American geographer, Karl Raitz (1995), has suggested that the 'sports landscape' consists of a variety of elements which make the overall sporting experience much more than watching a game. Gratification is increased, he suggests, from a variety of site elements that together create a pleasurable experience. Sports places may, therefore, come to have their own 'sense of place'. As I will show later, sentiment is of some importance when considering the possible re-location of sports facilities.

Sounds also contribute to a sense of place. Songs, chants, cheers and jeers contribute to the overall pleasure of a sports event. In his book *Fever Pitch* the Arsenal fan(atic) Nick Hornby (1992) referred to some of the sounds of the stadium: 'formal ritual noise', the 'spontaneous shapeless roars' and the 'vigour of the chanting'. In other sports integral sounds include national anthems, team songs and music that actually assists in the choreography of the of the event, as in ice skating. Smells also contribute to a sense of place. Sports smells are more than the odour of liniment wafting from changing rooms: cricket at Tunbridge Wells is linked to the scent of rhododendrons; and, for some, stale cigarette smoke is integral to watching football. The stimulation of the senses contributes to what have been called 'sensuous geographies'.

A home field advantage

The 'sense of place' can be related to one of the seemingly common phenomena of sports: the home team seems to have an advantage over the visiting team. Teams win more of their matches at home than away, and score more and concede less goals or points at home. This 'home field advantage' is illustrated by Table 1, which illustrates the number of home and away wins for British football clubs for the 1982-83 season.

What Table 1 shows is that during one season British football clubs won more games at home than away. However, it also reveals considerable differences in the apparent home field advantage between League divisions. In England, Division 1 seems to have the greatest home field advantage and the same is true in Scotland, though in Scotland the home/away ratio is much less. This kind of occurrence has been found in many sports.

Table 1: Examples of the home field advantage 1982-83. Source: Bale, 1989.

| League | Number of wins | | Home/away ratio |
	Home	Away	
Division 1	255	96	2.66
Division 2	220	98	2.24
Division 3	297	118	2.52
Division 4	283	127	2.23
Alliance Premier	247	102	2.42
Scottish Premier	83	51	1.63
Scottish Division 1	116	92	1.26
Scottish Division 2	121	85	1.42

A number of factors have been suggested to 'explain' the home field advantage and, as in many areas of geography, it is unlikely that a single factor can be used to explain such an occurrence. The kinds of reasons used to explain it are:

■ home support;
■ referee bias;
■ tiredness of visiting team resulting from travel to an away game;
■ unfamiliarity with the quirks of the playing field and arena by the visiting team.

It might be assumed, therefore, that if one sports site is exactly the same as any other, the home advantage will be less evident. However, it is in the most 'placeless' of sports – basketball and ice hockey – that the home field advantage has been found to be the greatest. This suggests that the presence of spectators, close to the action in a confined space, may be of great significance in 'explaining' the advantage of the home location in team sports. To investigate this phenomenon go to Activity Box 5.

The virtual stadium?

It could be argued that if teams and players are at an advantage when playing 'at home', then any individuality that the home ground has should be eliminated. Such individuality would include the spectators, whose presence, it seems, provides players with a home advantage. The philosopher Paul Weiss noted that:

> 'Ideally a normal set of conditions for a race is one in which there are no turns, no wind, no interference, no interval between starting signal and start, and no irregularities to the track – in short, no deviations from a standard situation' (Weiss, 1968, p. 105).

Although written in the context of a track event in athletics, the general idea is applicable to all sports. Weiss suggests that in such an environment there should be 'no interference'. This would suggest moving sports indoors to eliminate the effects of wind, rain, temperature, etc., and, presumably, interference from spectators. This may sound far-fetched but consider the views of Jean Baudrillard on the 'phantom' European Cup football match, played between Real Madrid and Naples on 16 September 1987. According to Baudrillard, this match which took

---

Activity Box 5: Investigating the home field advantage

1. Undertake an analysis of a team sport for British football in the late 1990s or early 2000s. Does a home field advantage exist? (Data on cricket and football can be found in *Wisden's Cricketers' Almanac* and *Rothman's Football Yearbook*. Other sports yearbooks also exist.)
2. In addition to home/away differences, consider the home/away differences in: (a) goals/points scored, and (b) goals/points conceded. Is there a home advantage here?
3. Compare the home advantage in one indoor sport (e.g. basketball, ice hockey) and one outdoor sport (e.g. rugby, football). Are there differences between the home advantage in indoor and outdoor events?
4. Look at the results of your own school's/local education authority's sports. Does a home field advantage exist for sports at the school level?
5. If possible, discuss what sports personnel (players, coaches, managers) think accounts for the home advantage (if it exists!).

Activity Box 6: Investigating spectator sport

Here are some points for discussion as a whole class:

1. To what extent are sports once played only out of doors today being 'interiorised'?
2. Debate the pros and cons about watching sport on television and watching it live.
3. Can the emotions and senses involved in watching live sport be reproduced while watching it on television in the home or a pub?
4. Does place matter when watching sport?

Figure 7: At 'Sluggers', a sports bar at Coralville, Iowa, USA, fans can watch sports of their choice on television, while eating and drinking. Photo: John Bale.

place in an empty stadium, the result of disciplinary measured imposed by UEFA against Madrid, was:

> 'a world where a "real" event occurs in a vacuum, stripped of its context and visible only from afar, televisually. Here we have a sort of surgically accurate pre-figurement of our future: events so minimal that they might well not take place at all – along with their maximal enlargement on screens. No one will have directly experienced the actual course of such happenings, but everyone will have received an image of them. A pure event, in other words, devoid of any reference to nature, and readily susceptible to replacement by synthetic images' (Baudrillard, 1993, pp. 79-80).

What Baudrillard seems to be predicting is a form of sport that is mainly televisual. It could be argued that we are already on the way to being dominated and domesticated by 'virtual sports'. These are basically simulations of reality which, for many people, are actually an improvement on reality itself. Indeed, television sport has been termed the 'defining reality' of sport. The fine detail of the close-up, the action replays and the different angles projected by television make it, for many people, a better and cheaper way of watching. The home or the pub (and in the USA the 'sports bar') become alternative venues for watching sports. Drenched in sporting motifs and memorabilia, they also tend to be 'men's' places, reminding us that much sport reflects traditional masculine views (Figure 7).

CHAPTER 3

SPORT IN THE CITY AND ITS REGION

Sports at the urban scale can be looked at in at least three ways. The first focuses on the spatial and environmental impact of sports facilities on the people living in the city as a whole and on those living in proximity to sports facilities such as stadiums and golf courses. The second concerns the relocation of clubs and their stadiums and the third the location of new sports facilities. Research into these three (inter-related) aspects draws mainly, but not exclusively, on what has been termed 'welfare geography': a geography that is concerned with fairness or even ethics. Studies of sport in the city can range from the impact of mega-events such as the Olympic Games to the influence of a golf course on local house prices and the effects on local residents of a Third Division football match.

The impact of sport facilities
Broadly speaking, sports facilities such as stadiums, sports arenas and golf courses can be viewed as generating either positive or negative effects. Such effects are known as 'spillovers' or 'externalities', because the effects are external to their source; they spill over from their points of origin. Consider, for example, the best-known kind of sports facility in many cities, the football stadium. This can be recognised as generating both positive and negative spillovers at the same time. Negative effects are considered unfair (even unethical) because they impose part of the costs of staging, say, a football match, on local residents. For example, the traffic congestion around a football ground prevents local residents from parking close to their homes. This imposes a 'cost' on them. Positive effects, on the other hand, could also be considered unfair because they provide a 'free ride' for certain people. An example would be the pub which increases its revenue on match days simply because it is near to the stadium at which a match is played.

   The theoretical basis of this kind of study comes from 'welfare geography' and lies in the notion of 'externality gradients'. These refer to the decline of both positive and negative effects with increasing distance from, in this case, the stadium. A simple representation of these effects is shown in Figure 8. The negative and positive spillovers are shown as lines – and + respectively. In theory, each of these might be expected to decline with distance away from the stadium (S) but the negative effects fall off more steeply than the positive. At distance SL, the positive effects of the stadium start to outweigh those of the negative effects. Beyond SN no negative spillovers are experienced at all. This suggests that people living in the zone SL suffer from their *proximity* to the stadium

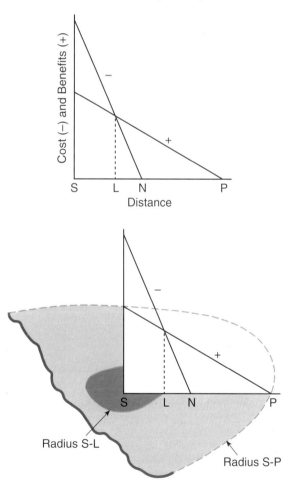

Figure 8: Spillover effects from a sports facility.

while those beyond it (if they are football fans) benefit from their *accessibility.* Those living within the radius SN have costs imposed on them, that they would otherwise not incur, by the presence of a sports event at S. Obvious examples of costs to local residents include congestion and queuing, e.g. at local shops, bus stops and train stations, the loss of sleep as a result of stadium noise or light. Unlike for example, replacing a pane of glass broken by a football hooligan, these examples cannot be 'costed' in money terms, but this in no way reduces their significance. In some cases the proximity to a sports facility may possess few, if any, negative spillovers. Proximity to a golf course, for example, is widely thought to enhance the quality of life, rather than detract from it, and may have a positive effect on property values.

Geographical approaches to the impacts of sports events explore two dimensions of such spillovers:

- the *geographical range* over which the stadium's impacts (positive and negative) are experienced, and
- the *kinds of impacts* sports events have on communities.

Negative effects

Studies into the spillover effects of sports facilities were prompted by the growth of football hooliganism in the 1970s. They sought to put hooliganism 'in its place', comparing it with other kinds of football-induced nuisances and seeing whether people living near stadiums found hooliganism of greater or lesser significance than other spillover effects. The general findings from a variety of such surveys showed that parked cars and traffic were the nuisances most commonly cited by people living in proximity to football stadiums (go to activity box 7). Hooliganism, though obviously very disturbing to individuals involved in its impact, was cited by a relatively small number of people living near (within 1.5km) the 37 grounds surveyed. Whereas 10 per cent of those interviewed claimed that football hooliganism was a nuisance, the respective figures for parked cars and traffic were 18 and 22 per cent. Only in a small number of cases was hooliganism mentioned by more people than cited parked cars and traffic.

Not surprisingly, nuisances were perceived to decline with distance from their sources (i.e. the stadiums – see Figure 9). But considerable variation existed between locations. For example, around

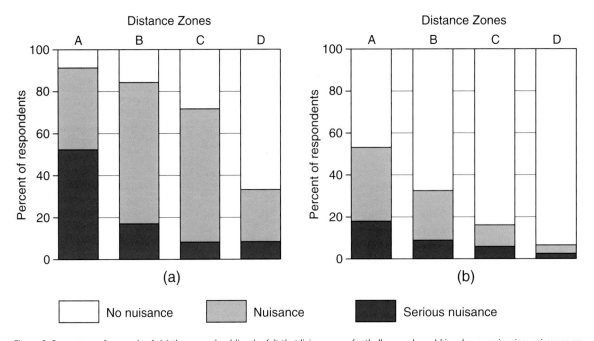

Figure 9: Percentage of a sample of: (a) the general public who felt that living near a football ground would involve experiencing nuisances on match days, and (b) residents living near football grounds who perceived football-related nuisances on match days. A-D represent 500m-wide concentric rings centred on the football ground. Source: Bale, 1990.

Activity Box 7: Investigating nuisance in the field

The aim of this investigation is to establish the nature and extent of nuisances around a sports stadium in your own (or the nearest) town.

1. **In the classroom:** On a local Ordnance Survey map (1:25 000) identify 150-200 residences, chosen by random point sampling, within 1.5km of a local sports stadium.
2. Number each point.
3. Draw three concentric circles around the stadium, each circle representing zones 500m from the stadium (500m, 1000m, 1500m). Approximately the same number of sample points should fall within each zone. (Ideally the number of points in each zone should be proportionate to the number of residences.)
4. **In the field:** In pairs, visit each sample residence, each of which is represented by a number on your base map.
5. On your interview schedule, make sure that you write the number representing the residence you are visiting.
6. Use the following interview schedule (or your own version of it) at each residence to discover the extent and nature of nuisances:
   a) Living here, do you feel that on average match days, when.................................. Club are playing at home (name stadium if necessary), any of the following are nuisances:
   b) Circle answers as appropriate.
      Traffic (Yes/No)
      Parked Cars (Yes/No)
      Pedestrians (Yes/No)
      Hooliganism/vandalism (Yes/No)
      Noise (Yes/No)
      Other (please specify)
   c) Are any of these serious nuisances? If so, underline as appropriate.

Possible additional questions
   d) Are you a fan of .... Club? (Yes/No)

After the interview
   e) Was the person who answered your question male ❏ or female ❏?
      Tick the appropriate age category of the person who answered your questions (do not ask how old they are!):
      Under 20 ❏   20-50 ❏   Over 50 ❏
7. **Back in the classroom** Count the number of respondents in each zone who replied 'Yes' to any of the items listed under 6b (i.e. who identified 'nuisances'). Score these '1' on the map at the appropriate points.
8. Count the number of respondents in each zone who identified **any of the items** listed under 6b as 'serious nuisance'. Score these '2' on the map at the appropriate points.
9. For each of the individual impacts listed in 6b, count the number of respondents in each zone who identified them as 'nuisances' or 'serious nuisances'.
10. What percentage of the total number of interviewees said that they perceived (i) 'nuisances' and (ii) 'serious nuisances' on match days?
11. What percentage of the total number of interviewees **in each zone** said that they perceived (i) 'nuisances' and (ii) 'serious nuisances' on match days?
12. Examine nuisance differences between the zones and construct graphs similar to those in Figure 9.
13. Identify the nature of the nuisances as perceived by local residents. Which were most frequently mentioned?
14. Write a report of your project, giving it a title of your choice.

Optional extra activities
1. Using the scores for each point on your base map, interpolate nuisance contours (contour values are 1 and 2, delimiting generalised areas of 'nuisance' and 'serious nuisance').
2. How far does the 'nuisance field' extend away from the source of nuisances?

Crewe Alexandra's ground hardly anybody perceived football as a 'serious nuisance'. Around Selhurst Park, however, where games were played every week because Crystal Palace and Wimbledon shared the ground, the percentage was much higher. Although such variations existed, a general finding of such surveys was that more people who did not live near a stadium were more likely to feel that they generated nuisances than people who actually did live near a stadium (see Figure 9). The stadium was therefore stigmatised by many people as a 'noxious' facility.

Positive effects

The positive effects of living within the extent of the positive spillover field (SP in Figure 8) derive from accessibility to the stadium. For example, fans living within an area close to a football stadium will pay less than those living beyond P to travel to a game. Also, some local retail outlets (pubs in particular) increase their revenues on match days. Evidence suggests that 27 per cent of retailers living within 1.5km of a sample of English football grounds increased their revenues on match days; only 8 per cent experienced a decrease, and most experienced no change. Local fans also experience 'psychic' benefits – the 'feel good factor' – when their club wins. There is also evidence of an increased work rate in local businesses following an important victory by a local team. Finally, the professional sports team provides free advertising for a city or town, though its value to the town will depend on the club's image – its success rate and so on.

Sports club re-location

In North America, the re-location of clubs in several team sports has been going on for many years, motivated mainly by the desire of owners to find new markets for their 'product'. There, franchises are commonly re-located at the continental scale, with moves taking place from the west to the east coast. In Britain, football has traditionally been run by non-profit motivated businesspeople – more as a hobby or as a means of entertaining business contacts – and re-location has been minimal. However, in recent years the number of football and other sports clubs seeking new locations for their stadiums has increased significantly. This desire for re-location may be attributed to the Taylor Report into the Hillsborough disaster in Sheffield where, in April 1989, almost 100 people were crushed to death when a surge of supporters entered an already full stand. The Taylor Report (1990) exposed the fact that football fans were being exploited in terms of spectating facilities, and that many stadiums were dangerous. The Report recommended a new breed of safe stadiums, ideally with ample car-parking facilities. It also recommended that the spectators in all stadiums, new or old, should be provided with seats: no standing space would be allowed.

Football clubs could respond to the Taylor Report in one of two ways: either by converting existing stadiums to provide seating for all or by building a completely new stadium in a new location. Converting a stadium to provide the lower-density spaces necessitated by the all-seater rule often meant increasing its height (e.g. in the case of both Manchester United and Liverpool football clubs). To do this, however, involved obtaining planning permission, often in the face of aggressive and vocal local opposition (see Information Box 3). Clubs who decided to relocate faced two different problems.

- First, as discussed earlier, stadiums have assumed the status of – or at least are perceived as – 'noxious facilities': things not desired in one's own back yard. Proximity to a stadium would, it is thought, lower the value of houses and face local residents with the negative spillovers from sports events. Thus, residents living near prospective stadium sites frequently oppose such developments with vocal and politically well-organised campaigns.

- Second, re-location has been found to be unpopular with fans. This relates to the 'topophilic' sentiment discussed earlier – the sentimental attachment of fans for their 'home' ground. Suburban re-location is also unpopular with planners, especially if it means eating up greenfield sites. On the other hand, brownfield, inner-urban locations have successfully accommodated new sports facilities and are cited as successful examples of urban regeneration. A relatively recent development in the British context has been the emergence of a nationally organised Federation of Stadium Communities which seeks to co-ordinate and assist local resident groups in campaigns against, or negotiations with, new stadium developments and expansions (see Information Box 3).

Information Box 3: Stadium expansion and local conflict

'The residents of Highbury (north London) will have the sympathy of people living in Blackburn, Leeds, Southampton and many other cities which are home to major football clubs. They have all been caught in the crossfire as soccer's Premiership giants seek to fit more bums on seats in a bid to ring extra cash through their till. As football becomes a multi-million pound business rather than a hobby, the pressure on clubs like Arsenal is to expand to fit in more supporters. But there is a problem with this. Like most football grounds in built-up areas Arsenal wants a stadium capable of seating 50 000 to replace the current 38 000-seater, but there is no way it can do this without affecting people living nearby.

Paul Weston of the Federation of Stadium Communities, which represents people living near sports grounds all over the country, said when there is a battle between football clubs and residents it is often the club which wins out because of its size and power:

"In Blackburn whole streets and communities were wiped away because the football club had to get bigger and wanted to expand its stadium" he said. "And in Southampton their ground is clearly not suitable for premier league football but the city did not want to lose the football club so a new site has been chosen but it is not suitable. But there is the emotive issue and a very tight bond between areas and their football clubs. Islington wants to keep hold of Arsenal, like Southampton wanted to keep its football team."

A planning brief, which gives guidelines on how Highbury stadium can be expanded, has been passed by Islington Council – and Mr Weston said that Arsenal was doing more than many other clubs to keep locals informed of its plans and take their views into account.

"We have some respect for the the fact that Arsenal and the council are prepared to take it step-by-step, rather than just jumping in head first. And thankfully they are going to consider other options like moving. But the whole community is very fearful of the whole situation and worried because Arsenal is so important."

He was impressed with the campaign the residents had mounted in their bid to ensure they did not suffer if the ground was expanded:

"There are a number of reasons for that," he said, "There is a mixture of people with skills and expertise living around the ground which you don't get everywhere and also they have been involved in previous battles."

Alison Carmichael, of the local residents' group, the Highbury Community Association said:

"the HCA thinks that the club's plans are too little and too late. On the one hand they say they need to keep up with the competition in order to be able to afford the best players, and on the other they say they do not want to do what all other top clubs are doing – turning their grounds into mega-entertainment centres bringing in millions of pounds."

Arsenal is working on an impact study which will consider the effect that expansion will have on the neighbourhood. Residents are determined not to give up until the final whistle.'
Source: http://www.interstae.co.uk/arseenalworld/forsale/080198.htm
Note: The residents' protest was successful and the football club is now considering a new location.

It is unwise to assume that all re-located and/or newly constructed stadiums do not create negative spillovers for local residents. A study of St Johnstone Football Club in Perth, Scotland, (Mason and Moncrieff, 1993) revealed that its negative externality field was of greater geographic extent than that of its former, city-centred ground (see also Calgary case study, page 25). To investigate the issues of re-locating a stadium, go to Activity Box 8.

The construction of new facilities

Not all new sports facilities are the result of the re-location of clubs: many are the result of increased demand for particular sports facilities. This is especially evident in the case of golf courses and for the Olympic Games – for which new facilities are being constructed in countries all over the world. The three case studies on pages 25 and 28-29 indicate how the construction of new facilities often impacts on humans and the environment.

Activity Box 8: A decision-making exercise

Introduction

You are to assume the role of a planning assistant who has almost completed a probationary year in the Portsmouth City Planning Office. As part of your work on re-location of Portsmouth Football Club's stadium you have to write a report for the City Planning Officer. In the Report section below you will find the formal tasks which you are required to complete.

Memorandum
Portsmouth City Planning Department

From: The City Planning Officer   **Date:** 6 June 1995
To: Rosemary Sharer   **Ref:** CPO/June/95

For the last part of your probationary year with Portsmouth City Planning Department I would like you to work on a proposed stadium development. The city football club is anxious to relocate its ground to a new stadium complex. While Portsmouth Football Club will be the main user, it is proposed to make it available for other events such as rock concerts. Included in the scheme are other profit-making enterprises such as retail outlets.

To help me judge how well your skills have developed since your arrival in the Planning Department, I would like you to complete the tasks shown in the Report below.

Three potential sites for a new stadium complex have been short-listed (see Item 1a-c on Figure 10). They are:

Site A: close to the existing stadium on a site owned by British Rail, at grid reference 658000;
Site B: on allotments in the north west of the city on a site owned by the City Council, at grid reference 640055;
Site C: on existing playing fields and rough, open ground to the north east, on a site owned partly by the City Council and partly by an independent school, at grid reference 680048.

Our newly elected councillors will appreciate an analysis of the town from the aerial photographs and maps (Items 1 and 2 in Figure 10). An enormous number of groups have stated an interest in the selection process. From what you know about them, I would like you to show how their viewpoints are likely to have an impact on their choice of site. After evaluating the suitability of the three sites, using a wide range of criteria and all the background information provided (see Figure 10), I would like you to recommend and justify your final choice of site to the Planning Committee.
Please remember that the City Council promotes nature conservation and the provision and maintenance of wildlife habitats and considers that there are particular opportunities at North Harbour. It is also a principal concern to safeguard the national and international importance of Langstone Harbour for nature conservation. No substantial development (or proliferation or consolidation of small-scale developments) which would significantly prejudice this interest will be permitted in the areas immediately adjoining the Harbour.

I hope that you find this a challenging task for your final piece of work.

Yours sincerely

David Washtenrub
City Planning Officer

■ **Activity Box 8: A decision-making exercise – continued**

Report

1. Annotate the outline map (Item 3). Provide a detailed description and evaluation of the environment and social character of the areas surrounding the three sites.
2. For each of the groups listed below, summarise the views you would expect it to hold with regard to the choice between the three sites:
   ■ National Rivers Authority
   ■ Royal Society for the Protection of Birds
   ■ Current landowners
   ■ Drayton and Farlington Residents' Association
   ■ Small Retailers Association
   ■ Department for Transport
   ■ Labour Party
   ■ Sports Council
3. Using appropriate criteria, evaluate the suitability of each site.
4. Which site would you recommend to the planning committee? Justify your choice.

■ **Case study 1: The Calgary Winter Olympics**

The Olympics can also have a negative impact on the local population as Olds' report on the 1998 Calgary Winter Olympics (in Canada) indicates (Information Box 4).

■ **Information Box 4: Housing impacts of the Winter Olympics**

'The Calgary Winter Olympics of 1998 caused or contributed to four forms of housing impact:

1. During the construction phase of the Games, a stadium was sited in a recreational area bordering one of Calgary's poorest residential communities, Victoria Park. The stadium was sited in this area against most of the community's wishes in a process which involved autocratic decision-making. This decision has contributed to the ongoing destabilisation of the community in order to satisfy future expansion plans for the recreational area – the Calgary Stampede and Exhibition grounds.
2. Approximately 740 tenants were displaced from two apartment building complexes in Calgary. The tenants were offered moving assistance and financial incentives to move, although it should be noted they had no legal choice as the 1988 Alberta Landlord and Tenant Act permits eviction without cause.
3. Several dozen long-term residential hotel dwellers were re-located from their rooms in a downtown hotel (with incentives again) in order to make room for Olympic visitors.
4. Approximately 1450 students were temporarily displaced from residences at two Calgary educational institutions. Again, assistance was offered to the students to help their move, though they had no choice but to do so.

Community resistance was ineffective in Victoria Park, and failed to develop in any significant manner in the other cases, mainly because of a lack of access to, and support from, politicians and Olympic organisers (groups with interlocking networks) who have long-term plans for the community's land. Moreover, provincial laws governing landlord and tenant relations enabled such displacement to take place, effectively annulling the reasoning behind the tenants' protests. This situation both reflects and contributes to the perception of tenants in Alberta as "second class citizens".'

Adapted from: Olds, no date.

Item 1: Vertical aerial photographs of (a) Site A, (b) Site B, and (c) Site C.

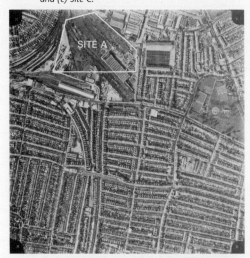

Item 2: A 1:50 000 Ordnance Survey map extract of the area (not shown)

Item 3: An outline map showing the wards of the city, the percentage of football supporters originating from various areas of the city and beyond, the location of sites of special scientific interest (SSSIs), nature reserves and the sites of potential new railway stations. This item is for annotation in Question 1.

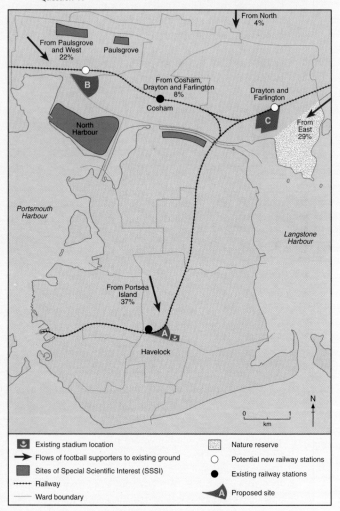

Item 5: Occupations of employed inhabitants in the wards surrounding the three sites

Type of employment	Site A (%)	Site B (%)	Site C (%)
Professional and managerial	14.60	5.58	18.66
Arts and sports	1.12	0.50	1.47
Scientific	7.10	5.17	6.22
Middle and junior management	9.53	5.76	13.10
Clerical	16.45	8.55	20.14
Personal services	24.32	29.87	17.67
Manufacturing	15.32	28.46	15.22
Construction and transport	9.16	11.95	6.21
Others	2.40	4.16	1.31

Item 4: Four social indicator maps (A-D), plus population pyramids of the three affected wards.

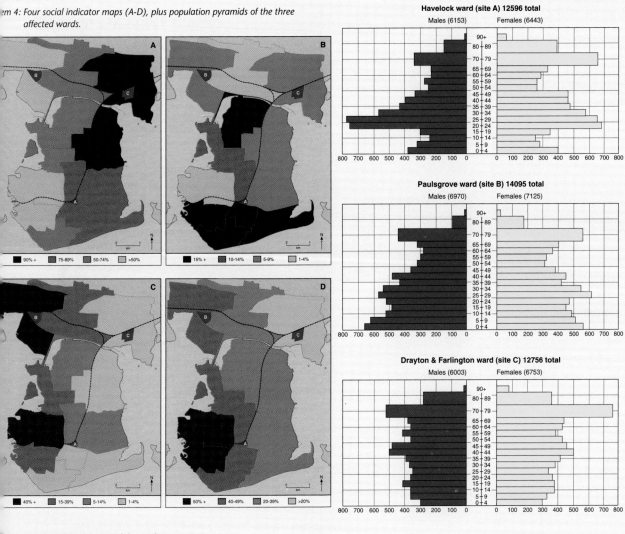

Havelock ward (site A) 12596 total
Males (6153)   Females (6443)

Paulsgrove ward (site B) 14095 total
Males (6970)   Females (7125)

Drayton & Farlington ward (site C) 12756 total
Males (6003)   Females (6753)

Item 6: An artist's impression of the stadium.

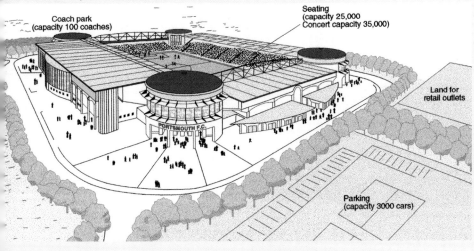

Coach park (capacity 100 coaches)

Seating (capacity 25,000 Concert capacity 35,000)

Land for retail outlets

PORTSMOUTH F.C.

Parking (capacity 3000 cars)

Figure 10: Resources for the decision making exercise in Activity Box 8.

Case study 2: Sydney and sustainability

Mega-sports events usually require new facilities. The growth of the Olympic Games over the last half-century means that staging a modern Olympics involves major urban planning and leads to debates about ethics, welfare and environment. True, the Olympic Games bring employment and status to the cities in which they are located, but they can also bring stigma if the cost becomes so great that local taxpayers are left paying the debts for years after the Games have finished. This was the case with the Montreal Olympics in 1978 and the World Student Games at Sheffield in 1991.

In recent years the notion of 'sustainability' has been applied to such mega-sports events, and the Sydney Summer Olympics of 2000 have been heralded as the most 'green' Games on record. Among 90 'sustainability' principles to which the Sydney planners signed up are:

- the maximum use of recycled and recyclable building materials;
- the widest possible use of renewable energy resources;
- the building of Olympic facilities on brownfield sites (see front cover);
- the maximum use of public transport;
- the maximisation of wastewater conservation and recycling;
- the minimum use of pesticides in landscape maintenance;
- the use of non-toxic paints, glues, varnishes, polishes, solvents and cleaning materials;
- the use of natural fibres for promotional clothing;
- the use of recycled paper for the printing of tickets;
- the use of non-disposable crockery by caterers;
- the use of electronic mail for communication.

Nevertheless, Sydney's green credentials have been criticised by some for not going far enough. It has been suggested, for example, that toxic waste in landfill sites occupied by Olympic facilities is far from safe, and that the expansion of Sydney Airport will result in increased noise and traffic pollution. (See Information Box 4 for other negative effects of the Olympic Games.)

Activity Box 9: Investigating the impact of international venues

1. Are there any sporting or cultural events (albeit at a smaller scale than the Olympics) in your home area that have negative or positive impacts on the host community?
2. Which groups in society are likely to benefit from the construction of Olympic, golfing or other international facilities and which are likely to be the losers?
3. Obtain information from organisers/managers about the impact of the event/facility on the environment. Is there any evidence to indicate that the organiser/manager is trying minimise the impact of the event/facility?
4. Suggest possible ways in which such events might be staged or facilities constructed and managed to overcome criticisms of their impact on the local population/environment.
5. Prepare a presentation on your findings.

Adapted from: Chalkley and Essex, 2000.

Case study 3: Golf courses

Golf course construction is not without controversy; the opposition to golf course development has been sufficient to lead to the establishment a Global Anti-Golf Movement, organised from Japan. Such opposition is mainly related to the negative environmental impacts of golf-course construction such as the application of chemicals and the denudation of forests and other ecosystems (see Information Box 5).

Not surprisingly, counter-arguments can be advanced in response to negative criticism. For example, it can be argued that golf courses, while putting considerable pressure on land in densely populated areas, nevertheless provide facilities that can be used all year round. It can also be argued that when golf courses are constructed on what was formerly poor quality agricultural land, the environment is enhanced, not simply in a visual sense but also in terms of greater diversity of habitat. Yet, together with skiing, golf is the sport that is subjected to most ecological critique.

Information Box 5: Golf and pollution

'Golf is wildly popular these days, and developers, anxious to cash in on the boom, are building new golf courses around the world. There are now 25 000 golf courses on the planet, 14 000 of them in the United States, and hundreds more are on the drawing board.

Today's perfectly manicured rolling green courses require massive amounts of land, water, and chemicals. Most US courses use 1500 pounds [680kg] of pesticides a year; that's seven times the amount used by farmers. Add to that a laundry list of fertilizers, herbicides, fungicides and other chemicals. And when it rains, it pours: runoff from golf courses has contaminated nearby groundwater, lagoons, lakes and wetlands.

Many of the resource-gobbling playlands are being built in South East Asia, where the thirst of national governments for foreign exchange has combined with the hunger of Japanese developers for paradisiacal sites. For Japan's 12 million golf fanatics, a shortage of land and soaring golf club membership costs – as high as US$250 000 a year – mean that it is often easier and cheaper to fly to Thailand or Malaysia. Thailand alone has 160 courses, with many more in the offing. Developers have set their sights on Vietnam, Laos, and Burma as well.

Too often, these new golf-resort developments are forcing people from their land. Developers who have trouble getting local people to sell sometimes buy up all the surrounding plots and deny them access to their land. Ninety acres is the minimum area needed to build the average course, and, since most new courses, especially in less developed countries, are developed as packages with luxury homes and other recreational amenities, a single project can cover up to 700 acres [1730ha].

The owners of these courses are also diverting precious water resources to keep their fairways green. In Indonesia, a major drought in 1994 caused wells to run dry, and farmers were not able to plant a second crop. However, Jakarta's golf courses continued to receive 1000 m^3 of water per course per day – enough to meet the daily needs of 1000 families.'

Adapted from: Roberts, 2000.

CHAPTER 4

SPORTS AT THE NATIONAL SCALE

Regional differences

It will be obvious to most people that the emphasis placed on sports varies from place to place. In the popular imagination some places might be identified as 'rugby regions', and others as 'football regions'. Attempts to 'objectively' identify geographical differences in sporting attributes have been a major feature of sports-geographic studies since the early 1940s. These studies use quantitative methods to identify differences in a range of sporting characteristics – for example, how the provision of sports facilities varies from place to place or how geographical differences exist in the regional 'production' of professional or elite sports participants. A second approach is to explore those sports geographies which reside inside people's heads. This approach reflects a shift in emphasis towards qualitative 'textual' studies rather than quantitative (number crunching) ones. This chapter explores various ways of looking at sport at the national scale.

Geographical studies of regional variations in sports facilities are obviously valuable for planning and marketing purposes because they identify areas that are under-provided with facilities as well as those that possess above the national level of provision. The identification of geographical differences in where sports participants come from may be based on club membership or on elite or professional sport participants. In each of these kinds of study, results are presented at absolute and relative (that is, per capita) terms. Central to many of these studies is the mapping of their results, usually displayed as choropleth maps (e.g. Figure 11). These kinds of studies are encouraged by the vast amount of statistical data generated by sports and remain relevant both academically and for use in the recruiting strategies of professional sports clubs. However, these approaches have been criticised because they demonstrate a style in which description takes priority over interpretation.

The approach to identifying sports regions illustrated in Figure 11 is based on the pioneering approach of the American geographer, John Rooney

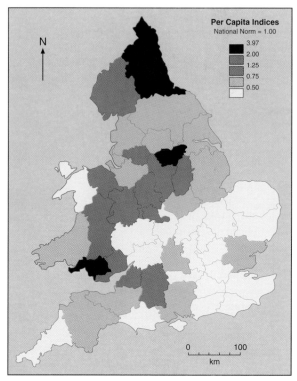

Figure 11: Per capita variation in the 'production' of professional football players, England and Wales, 1950. Source: Bale, 1983.

(1974), and shows the geographical variations in the birthplaces of professional footballers playing in Football League clubs in England and Wales in 1950. The idea of the per capita index is outlined in Information Box 6. In the case of Figure 11, an index of 1.00 represents the national per capita level of production of professional footballers. Higher scores reveal counties producing professional footballers at above the national norm. Figure 11 shows that these high scoring counties (producing at between two and four times the national norm) are overwhelmingly in the north of England; those 'producing' at below the per capita norm are in the south east. Particularly prominent are the contiguous group of high scoring counties in the north east of England and south Wales, suggesting some kind of 'football culture' in those regions. The study went on to show how, by

Information Box 6: The per capita index and specialisation indexes

In the context shown in Figure 11, the per capita index can be calculated by using the following formula:

$$I = \frac{(N/p)}{(1/n)}$$

Where I is the per capita index of player 'production';
N is the number of players 'produced' in a given area (i.e. county);
p is the population of that area;
n is the number of people per player 'produced' in the area as a whole.

For example, if the area had a population of 900 000 and 'produced' 20 players, N/P = 20/900 000; and one player for every 23 000 of the national population 1/n = 1/23 000. The formula would be

$$I = \frac{(20/900\ 000)}{(1/23\ 000)} = 0.51$$

The national per capita index is always 1.00. An area (county or region) with an index of 2.00 would be 'producing' at twice the national average, one with an index of 0.5 at half the national average.

In multi-event sports like athletics or swimming, the per capita measure of 'production' should arguably be complemented by a measure of diversification. A nation's or region's sports 'production' may be diversified or specialised. A specialisation index (SI) can be calculated by applying the following formula:

$$SI = \sqrt{p1^2 + p2^2 + p3^2 \dots\dots pn^2}$$

Where p1 is the percentage of the total number of athletes in event 1
p2 the percentage in event 2, etc.
The maximum score is always 100, indicating extreme specialisation with all athletes in one event. The lowest score, with the same percentage in each event, will depend on the number of events

1980, there had been a reduction in the polarisation of player production and that the high levels found in the north east had declined while the levels found in the south east in 1950 had increased.

Other geographical aspects of sports at the national scale have included the migration of sports talent and the shifting centres of success in team sports. In the UK, for example, it has been shown that the dominant migration flow of professional footballers has been from north to south. It has also been shown that the 'centre of gravity' of the Football League (the 'average' location of clubs) has been shifting south-eastwards in the last 100 years. Geographical work has also tried to show where professional sports teams ought to be located, according to the principles of central place theory.

Activity Box 10: Constructing mental sports maps

1. On an outline map of Britain or the British Isles, that includes counties and major towns and cities, superimpose a grid with each square representing an area of about 50km x 50km.
2. Using a set of five such maps, one for each of five sports, undertake a survey of about 50 people (the exact number is not important). Ask them to identify the areas in 10 (or fewer) squares on each map that they identify with, for example, those sports shown in Figure 12 or horse racing, athletics, etc.
3. Construct a composite map for cricket, recording the percentage of respondents who identified the sport with each square. For example, if every respondent identified cricket with the square in which Kent is located, that square would have a score of 100; if half the respondents identified Lancashire, its square would have a score of 50.
4. Repeat this for each of the other sports.
5. For each map construct a choropleth map to illustrate regional differences in the strength of image of each sport.
6. For each map attempt to convert your data into a series of generalised isolines (see, e.g. Figure 12).
7. Produce an aggregate map as in Figure 12.

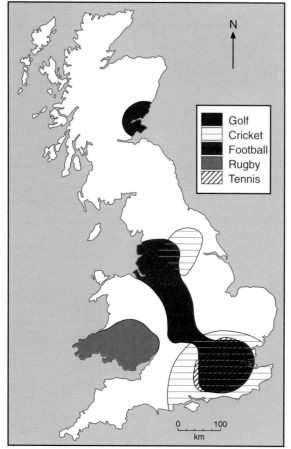

Figure 12: A mental map of cricket, football, golf, rugby and tennis.
Source: Bale, 1989.

Sport and the geographical imagination

Mental maps

In sports geography, mental maps have been used to identify collective perceptions of sport and place. Figure 12 is an example of such a mental map which, in this case, relates to people's perceptions of the locations of five sports in England, Wales and Scotland. The shaded areas on the map define the areas which 60 per cent of a group of respondents associated with each sport. Mental maps are the result of a number of stimuli that have cumulatively led people to associate sport with place. Knowledge of such images may be of value to the respective regions for publicity or advertising purposes, projecting themselves as 'virile' regions as a result of their sporting associations.

Imaginative geographies

Imaginative geographies are less 'innocent' than mental maps and seek to reveal the way in which sport-place images are constructed by texts such as novels, poems, and visual arts such as painting, photography or the cinema. The 'imaginative geography' of cricket can be explored by an excavation (digging beneath the surface) of the kinds of texts noted above. Before doing so, it is worth noting that cricket contains all the characteristics of modern, technologised sport that have been mentioned earlier (see pages 9-14): it is highly quantified, geometricised and bureaucratised (page 10) and the surfaces on which it is played are scientifically tended (page 14); it also happens to be played throughout England, from the northern industrial cities to the southern suburbs.

The following three texts on imagined geographies each convey a particular attitude to cricket. First, an extract from Edmund Blunden's poem, *The Season Opens*, written in the 1930s (quoted in Ross, 1981, p. 405):

'A tower we must have, and a clock in the tower,
Looking over the tombs, the tithe barn,
the bower;
The inn and the mill, the forge and the hall,
And the loamy sweet meadow that loves bat
and ball.'

Second, an extract from A.G. Macdonell's *England, Their England*, which describes a cricket ground in Kent:

'It was a hot summer's afternoon. There was no wind, and the smoke from the red-roofed cottages curled slowly up into the golden haze. The clock on the flint tower of the church struck the half-hour, and the vibrations spread slowly across the shimmering hedgerows. ... The cricket field itself was a mass of daisies and buttercups and dandelions, tall grasses and purple vetches and thistle-down, and great clumps of dark-red sorrel, except, of course, for the oblong patch at the centre – mown, rolled, watered – a smooth, shining emerald of grass, the Pride of Fordenden, the Wicket' (Macdonell, 1933, p. 107).

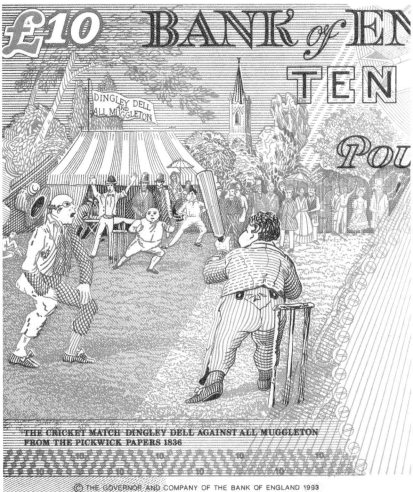

Figure 13: Sport on an English £10 note.
© The Bank of England.
Reproduced with permission

Third, the back of an English £10 bank note shows an image of a cricket match between Dingley Dell and All Muggleton (Figure 13), taking place in Dingley Dell (from Charles Dickens's novel *The Pickwick Papers*).

These can be seen as typical representations (or re-presentations) of the English cricket landscape.

I would suggest they have two particular features in common.

1. They communicate images of the picturesque and the rural. The background to cricket in Blunden's verse is the church, the inn, the tithe-barn; all are allusions to the rural. This is the imagined 'landscape ensemble' noted earlier. Such soothing images can be read as acting as an antidote to the

---

Activity Box 11: Excavating paintings

Look at the two paintings shown in Figures 14 and 15.

1. Attempt an 'excavation' of these images and speculate about what they are saying about the cultural geography of British football and horse racing.
2. Recall any television plays or other visual media that centre on sports. Do they carry any connotations of place, region or social class?

depression of 1930s England. Representations of cricket on the village green continue to promote such images in a wide range of contexts, from coffee-table books to the selling of motor cars. Nostalgia for 'Merrie England' can be fostered through such images and even cricket at the highest level is often represented as picturesque and 'English'. Photographs of first-class matches at Worcester invariably include the imposing Gothic cathedral as a backdrop.

2. They construct a kind of southern-ness. The Macdonell quotation is explicitly set in Kent and hardly carries connotations of northern, industrial England. The £10 note shows a rural scene, with the church and trees clearly presented, and being on a Bank of England note it is also seen to signify England. And it was the national cricket team that people supported that acted as the criterion which some politicians would regard as *the* test of one's nationality.

These images place cricket in a particular kind of environment and location. They also construct a reassuring and ordered image of 'Englishness' – an Englishness a million miles away from inner-city riots, violent demonstrators against capitalism, squalor, racial strife, unemployment, lager louts and other depressing aspects of English life. The images hark back to a mythical golden age, an 'imagined

Figure 14: *Going to the Match* by L.S. Lowry.
© Professional Footballers' Association. Reproduced with permission.

community' or mythical idyll, hence serving an ideological purpose. The identification of 'imagined sports communities' is also possible at the global scale where particular 'sporting nations' can be textually constructed, providing images that reflect national virility. Other representations of sporting activities (see Figures 14 and 15) and their relation to cultural geography are shown in Activity Box 11.

Figure 15: *Derby Day* (oil on canvas) by William Powell Frith (1819-1909) (after). Bonhams, London, UK/Bridgeman Art Library.

CHAPTER 5

SPORT AND ITS GLOBAL SYSTEM

Sport is a kind of international 'currency' in the sense that its rules and regulations are understood by a very wide variety of peoples all over the world. The number of nations affiliated to the International Amateur Athletics Association, for example, is over 200. Sports are ultimately regulated by international bureaucracies, that is non-government organisations whose decisions can sometimes over-ride those of national governments. Much sport-associated business, too, is global in its organisation. Consider, for example, the case of sportswear companies such as Nike, Adidas, Reebok or Puma. Such trans-national corporations may be controlled from the west but many of their manufacturing operations are carried out in so-called 'third world' countries. A further aspect of sport, which is global in character, is the movement of sport-labour from country to country. One only has to look at the variety of national origins of players in the English and Scottish Premier League football clubs to appreciate that sports stars are among the most geographically mobile of labour forces.

The growth of global sport

Sport in its modern form (i.e. achievement sport) was basically a European innovation that, in the space of a little more than a century, became adopted in most countries of the world. It was diffused, mainly from England, by a wide variety of 'carriers' who exported it with various motives in mind. In this respect, sport was not homogenous. Some sports were passed on to local élites while others were almost thrust upon the masses. The adoption of sport as an innovation is, perhaps, most graphically illustrated by the period of colonialism in the late nineteenth and early twentieth centuries. Among the first facilities built in many colonial cities were cricket pitches, golf courses and tennis courts for the recreational use of the colonial élites. In Asia golf was established by British colonials; exemplar venues being the Royal Calcutta, the Royal Hong Kong and Kobe clubs for diplomats, businessmen (the noun is deliberately gendered) and the military hierarchy. Similar projects were developed in colonial Africa. The landscapes of sport were as much imperialist projects as the railways, ports and residences constructed by agents of the Empire.

At the same time, sport was being introduced to native peoples with a different purpose in mind. In early twentieth century Kenya, for example, a missionary noted that:

> **'The game of football, played in the afternoon, was played for moral benefit as much as recreational relief ... to stiffen the backbone of these African boys by teaching them manliness, good temper and unselfishness – qualities amongst others which have done much to make a Britisher' (quoted in Bale and Sang, 1996, p. 77).**

This was the ethos of 'muscular Christianity'. Participation in 'manly' English sports served as a form of social control, keeping 'the natives' out of trouble, just as they had kept schoolboys under control in early nineteenth century England. Today the ambition of global sports organisations and businesses is to spread western sports into all countries of the world, a graphic example of neo-colonialism (see page 41).

In much colonial writing 'the African' was presented as being a 'natural athlete', a myth that has been sustained to the present day. Such a myth was paradoxically positioned next to another myth – that the African was lazy and idle. Geographers were complicit in such myth-making through the widely assumed theory of environmental determinism – the idea that human behaviour was overwhelmingly related to the physical environment. One of the main proponents of the theory was the American geographer Ellsworth Huntington. Huntington prepared maps of the world showing that most of Africa, for example, was a region of low 'climatic efficiency', the nations therein having low 'indexes of vigour' (Huntington, 1945). This led many sports scientists to assume that while Africans may have an innate 'jungle instinct' (a term used in a sports-geography dissertation from the 1950s) that made them good sprinters, they lacked the vigour to become long-distance runners. This myth was shattered during the 1960s when runners from Ethiopia and Kenya first achieved world-class performances (Bale and Sang, 1996). Racial, physical-environmental and genetic explanations of sports success are today widely rejected and national sports prowess is thought to result from a large number of different factors.

The growth of world sports has not produced an even distribution of sports participation at the global scale, however. In the case of achievement sport, the West tends to dominate the rest of the world in terms of numbers of participants, the provision of facilities and sporting success. Some Olympic sports hardly exist in some 'third world' countries, simply because they are capital intensive. The cost of participation at even a modest level in sports like yachting, skiing or motor racing is prohibitive to all but the most affluent. Participation in sports like golf or tennis can be correlated with affluence though there are, of course, always exceptions. Where state funding has been fed in, poorer countries can assume global significance in particular sports. For example, in 1980 East Germany 'produced' over 32 times the global average number of world class swimmers ('world class' is defined as

having achieved a performance good enough to be in the top 100 in the world in an Olympic event). A graphic example of the global imbalance in sports is shown in Figure 16. This cartogram (sometimes called a 'topological map') shows the size of countries proportional to the number of world-class track and field athletes they produced in 1992. Each country is shaded according to its per capita index (see page 32). The world is clearly top-heavy. Note the size, in terms of 'track and field space', of South America and Asia, and the size of Cuba both in absolute and per capita terms. It is also important to notice what is not on the map: for example, the relatively small number of countries shown in South America and Asia reminds us of the fact that many countries in the world 'produce' no world-class athletes.

From the broad pattern shown in Figure 16 it may be possible to find some association between gross national product per capita and sports success per capita. Equally, it might be possible to find apparent associations with climatic variables. But it is dangerous to jump to conclusions. In Figure 16 Kenya apparently has a relatively high per capita level of athlete 'production' while Ethiopia, its northern neighbour, has a much lower level. The altitude factor is often claimed to be the explanation for the apparent

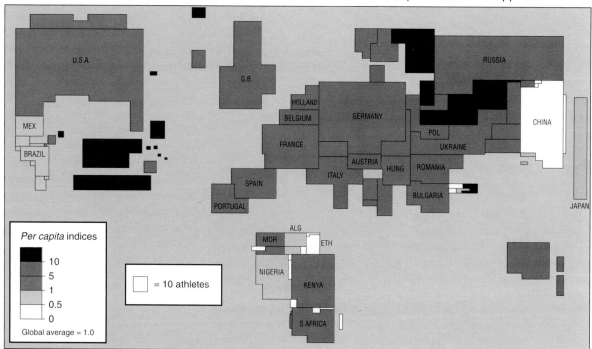

Figure 16: The world 'athletics space' in 1992. Source: Bale and Sang, 1996

success of these countries in producing world-class long distance runners, but, despite similarities in their relief, the countries differ greatly in their per capita output. Historical and cultural factors should never be ignored when working towards an explanation of such geographical variations.

A tendency for much of the twentieth century was for the West to colonise the rest of the world with their sporting practices. In recent decades there has been something of a counter-trend of non-Western sports being adopted in Western countries. Judo is perhaps the classic example but the Indian game of *kabbadi* (a game played on a pitch the size of a a badminton court and likened to a mixture of wrestling, tag and rugby) is also diffusing rapidly: it is now popular in Nepal, Bangladesh, Sri Lanka, Japan, Pakistan, USA, UK and Canada.

The international movements of sports labour
It was noted earlier that sport was introduced to some colonial nations as a form of social control. But this was not the only reason for introducing sports to the colonies. By the 1930s it was becoming clear to many colonial powers that 'the African', for example, could be readily 'transformed' or 'converted' into a modern athlete. French sporting authorities, disappointed with their failure to win many medals at the 1936 Berlin Olympics, and seduced by the apparent 'superman' status of African Americans such as Jesse Owens, undertook to do fieldwork in Africa in the hope of finding what they perceived to be 'natural athletes'. These, it was hoped, would bolster the French team. The scouring of the world for athletic and sporting talent continues to the present day. (Go to Activity Box 12.)

Sports labour migration takes a variety of forms at the present time, and involves different categories of 'migrant'. These include:

1. **Returnees** – those who travel to compete overseas but return to their homes immediately afterwards. This would be the traditional type of short-term migration to fulfil what amounts to a working obligation, such as playing in an international tennis match or competing in the Olympic Games. In such cases, the overseas sojourn in brief, taking up a day or two at least and a month at most.
2. **Mercenaries** – those who migrate to a foreign country for longer term sports-work, perhaps for several years. They include rugby league players from Australia and New Zealand (and many other countries) who play rugby in England and Wales and vice versa. Also included are student-athletes, large numbers of whom spend a number of years in universities and colleges in the USA on 'sports scholarships'. Nearly 16 per cent of American football players in the major US colleges are foreign recruits. In some cases, this form of migration has caused serious problems of defining who is, and who is not, eligible to compete for particular nations and raises interesting questions of national identity and affiliation. Such people become multi-national as well as multi-cultural. For example, the German cyclist, Jan Bratkowski (see front cover), rides for the American team Manheim, and Wilson Kipketer, the world 800m record holder, was brought up in Kenya, became a citizen of Denmark, lives in Italy for much of the year, and is sponsored by a German sports-shoe company. Given such a mix of national affiliations it is unclear who he is representing.
3. **Nomadic cosmopolitans** – those who reside for short periods of time in a large number of different global locations. Grand Prix racing drivers typify such sports workers, raising questions about what is meant by 'identity' in a sports context. It could be argued that the prime objective of sports-workers is to maximise their revenues. To do this might bring them into conflict with the national

Activity Box 12: Investigating the world of footballers

Using data contained in the annual edition(s) of *Rothman's Football Yearbook*, identify the origins (i.e. birthplaces and nations) of 'imported' footballers to the UK.

1. Which regions supply the majority of professional footballers?
2. Speculate about possible explanations for any patterns of player origins.
3. Look for correlations between these, Figure 16 and the information given on pages 35-40. Offer explanations for any patterns you discover.

federations that run their sport and feel that national representation should come first. Could 'nomadic cosmopolitan' sports workers be representing commercial interests rather than their nations? Are racing drivers in this category no longer representing nations but car firms? Such a model of representation could, in the future, characterise more sports.

By the end of the twentieth century, it was possible to find some English Premier League football teams in which 11 players had been imported from overseas countries. Twenty years earlier, to have a foreign player on a team would have been a novelty. The migration of sports labour between countries of the European Community is not subject to any restrictions. However, opposition to free movement is sometimes opposed by the lower divisions who see the gulf between rich and poor clubs growing greater

by the year. The lower division clubs and the players' union often suggest that there should be a ban or limit on the number of imported players. However, such a ban would contravene European Union laws governing the free movement of labour within the EU.

The migration of talent is aided by talent-scouts and agents whose task is to scour the world for sports labour. A recent outcome of such talent spotting has been the development of pipelines between various African countries and those in Europe, as a result of which many talented people from the African continent now work for European sports organisations. A more sinister side to such migration is that young boys are lured to Europe with the prospect of gaining fame and fortune as, for example, football players in big clubs. In some instances they have been rejected and, after a relatively short period of time, have become street children in cities such as Brussels.

Information Box 7: The cost of a pair of shoes

The information in the table below was compiled in 1995 by researchers at the *Washington Post* newspaper using information from Nike, the US Customs Service, a large national retail chain, the Athletic Footwear Association, industry consultants and executives. It provides a breakdown of the costs involved in producing a pair of Nike 'Air Pegasus' shoes (whose retail price was then US$70). (Other researchers have done similar breakdowns and come up with much the same result.)

	US$		US$		US$
Production labour	2.75	Research and development	0.25	Retailer's rent	9.00
Materials	9.00	Promotion and advertising	4.00	Personnel	9.50
Rent, equipment	3.00	Sales, distribution, admin	5.00	Other	7.00
Supplier's operating profit	1.75	Nike's operating profit	6.25	Retailer's operating profit	9.00
Duties (taxes)	3.00	**Cost to retailer**	**35.50**	**Cost to consumer**	**70.00**
Shipping	0.50				
Production cost	**20.00**				

If such shoe firms increased their wages by a small amount the impact on their profits would be minimal. In 1995 the cost of production labour was only US$2.75 or 4 per cent of the price paid by the consumer. So wages for production workers could have been increased significantly without adding much to the cost of the shoes. Even if wages had been doubled and the extra cost passed straight on to the consumer, it would have added no more to the price of the shoes than the cost of a pair of shoelaces. Consumers would hardly have noticed, but it would have made an enormous difference to hundreds of thousands of production workers and their families.

Note that Nike spent nearly twice as much on promotion and advertising as it did on production workers' wages. In March 1995, for example, tennis star Andre Agassi was paid a reputed Au$140 million to promote Nike shoes and clothing.

However, the consumer is placed in a difficult position in responding with any kind of 'action' on a manufacturer's exploitation of labour in poor nations. To stop buying particular brands of sportswear might signify a form of protest but it might also lead to labour lay-offs.

Source: http://www.caa.org.au/campaigns/nike/sweat2.html#OneH

The sports goods industry

The sports goods industry provides a good example of how the global may be found in the local. I have already alluded to the global bureaucracies that administer sports and to the global flows of sports-workers. We only have to look at the advertising icons in the modern stadium and the sports goods in our local sportswear outlets to see the global in our own localities. Consider geographer Allan Pred's description of Stockholm's multi-purpose 'facility', appropriately called the 'Globe'. He describes it as:

> **'a market-place (yet another metaphor for the stadium) where commodified bodies are used to market other commodities, where the jerseys and pants of ice-hockey players are covered with advertisements for global firms that market cars and household electronic goods in Sweden (Opel, Pioneer), with advertisements for Swedish firms that globally market steel, cars, trucks, food products and insurance, with the advertisements of Swedish retail chains and coffee firms with global sources. The Globe [is a] showplace where athletic performers become little more than sandwich-board carriers – modern counterparts to those plodding downtrodden individuals who were once a common sight on downtown streets – and at the same time become somewhat akin to prostitutes, being commodities and sellers at once' (Pred, 1995, p. 203).**

In other words, the aptly named Globe represents sport as part of the global economic system.

Nike, Brooks and New Balance, for example, are American sports goods manufacturers whose products are sold all over the world. Nike, in particular, has become a global icon with its 'Swoosh' logo and its slogan 'Just do it' being identifiable from Sunderland to Sao Paulo. You may be less aware, however, that Nike shoes and other sports goods such as footballs, cricket balls and sports clothing are not, in fact, made in the country where the company has its headquarters. The sports footwear industry, including German companies such as Adidas and Puma, illustrate the role of global subcontracting and flexibility in sports goods production. In fact, much 'sports' footwear has moved beyond having anything to do with sport and might be better described as 'leisure wear' (even 'fashion wear'), for which there is a huge global market. Many people now buy sports shoes for their 'image value', not their use value; it is the label that counts.

In order to keep costs low, many such shoe and equipment companies sub-contract the manufacture and assembly of their products to what have been called 'global sweatshops', that is low-cost labour economies in the Far East. True, international sports goods corporations bring employment to poor countries. However, wages and conditions for workers are poor, child labour often being exploited in poor working conditions. Employment costs make up a small fraction of the eventual price of a pair of sports shoes (see Information Box 7) and considerable amounts are spent on marketing and advertising.

Final thoughts

Selecting sport as a subject to be studied provides the chance to explore something that is often taken for granted and treated in a commonsense kind of way. This book shows that there is more to sport than this. Indeed, in the words of sports sociologist, John Loy 'studying sport is often as much fun as playing sport and on occasion just as serious' (1975, p. vii). These words resonate in the geography of sport today, just as they did then.

Selected websites

- Anti-Nike: http://www.caa.org.au/campaigns/nike/sweat2.html#OneH
- Bread not Circuses: http://www.breadnotcircuses.org/home.html – a coalition of groups concerned about Toronto's 2008 Olympic bid. This site contains many useful and interesting articles about the pros and cons of sporting mega-events.
- Cafod: http://www.cafod.org.uk/yttrainers.htm – similar to the anti-Nike site but more general and more education-oriented.
- Sir Norman Chester Centre for Football Research http://www.le.ac.uk/snccfr/research/fofs.html – an excellent site from Leicester University. Though football-related, it contains many useful ideas and helpful information, including fact sheets on sports-related subjects.
- US Golf Association: http://www.usga.org/green/index.html – provides an industry view of golf and the environment. Have a look at their 'Environment Education Program' and the variety of downloadable reports and articles.

References

Adams, R. (1995) 'Golf' in Raitz, K. (ed) *The Theater of Sport.* Baltimore: Johns Hopkins University Press, pp. 231-69.

Bale, J. (1983) 'Changing regional origins of an occupation: the case of professional footballers in 1950 and 1980', *Geography*, 68, 2, pp. 140-8.

Bale, J. (1989) *Sports Geography.* London: E&FN Spon.

Bale, J. (1990) 'In the shadow of the stadium: football grounds as urban nuisances', *Geography*, 75, 4, pp. 325-34.

Bale, J. and Sang, J. (1996) *Kenyan Running: Movement culture, geography and global change.* London: Frank Cass.

Baudrillard, J. (1993) *The Transparency of Evil.* London: Verso.

Brohm, J-M. (1978) *Sport: A prison of measured time.* London: Ink Links.

Chalkley, B. and Essex, S. (1999) 'Sydney 2000: the "green games"?', *Geography*, 84, 4, pp. 299-307.

Chalkley, B. and Essex, S. (2000) 'Learning from the Olympic Games', *Teaching Geography*, 25, 3, pp. 112-8.

Eichberg, H. (1998) *Body Cultures.* London: Routledge.

Foucault, M. (1979) *Discipline and Punish: The history of the prison.* London: Penguin.

Hornby, N. (1992) *Fever Pitch.* London: Gollancz.

Huntington, E. (1945) *Mainsprings of Civilisation.* New York: Mentor Books.

Klein, B. (1999) 'Cultural links: an international political economy of golf course landscapes' in Martin, R. and Miller, T. (eds) *SportCult.* Minneapolis: University of Minnesota Press, pp. 211-26.

Lowry, P. (1983) *Green Cathedrals.* Reading MA: Addison-Wesley.

Loy, J. (1975) 'Foreword' in Ball, D. and Loy, J. (eds) *Sport and Social Order.* Reading MA: Addison/Wesley, p. v-vii.

MacDonell, A.G. (1933) *England, Their England.* London: Macmillan.

Mason, C. and Moncrieff, A. (1993) 'The spatial externality fields of football stadia: the case of St Johnstone Fooball Club', *Scottish Geographical Magazine*, 109, pp. 96-105.

Olds, K. (no date) 'Urban mega-events; evictions and housing: the Canadian case', http://www.breadnotcircuses.org/kris_olds_toc.html

Pred, A. (1995) *Recognizing European Modernities.* London: Routledge.

Rail, G. (1998) 'Seismography of the postmodern condition' in Rail, G. (ed) *Sport and Postmodern Times.* Albany NY: State University of New York Press, pp. 150-1.

Raitz, Karl (ed) (1995) *The Theater of Sport.* Baltimore: John Hopkins University Press.

Rigauer, B. (1981) *Sport and Work.* New York: Columbia University Press.

Roberts, E. (2000) 'Golf war syndrome: how playing 18 holes endangers the Earth', http://utne.com

Rooney, J. (1974) *A Geography of American Sport: From Cabin Creek to Anaheim.* Reading MA: Addison-Wesley.

Ross, A. (ed) (1981) *The Penguin Cricketers Companion.* Harmondsworth: Penguin.

Scott Jenkins, V. (1994) *The Lawn: A history of an American obsession.* Washington DC: Smithsonian Institute Press.

Sillitoe, A. (1961) *The Loneliness of the Long Distance Runner.* London: Grafton.

Taylor, Lord Justice (1990) *The Hillsborough Disaster: Final report.* London: HMSO.

Tuan, Y-F. (1974) *Topophilia.* Englewood Cliffs NJ: Prentice Hall.

Tuan, Y-F. (1984) *Dominance and Affection: The making of pets.* New Haven: Yale University Press.

Wagner, P. (1981) 'Sport: culture and geography' in Pred, A. (ed) *Space and Time in Geography.* Lund: Gleerup.

Weiss, P. (1969) *Sport: A philosophical enquiry.* Carbondale IL: Southern Illinois University Press.

Further reading

Bale, J. (1981) 'Geography, sport and geographical education', *Geography*, 66, 2, pp. 104-15.

Bale, J. (1993) *Sport, Space and the City.* London: Routledge.

Bale, J. (1994) *Landscapes of Modern Sport.* Leicester: Leicester University Press.

Giulianotti, R. (1999) *Football: A sociology of the global game.* Cambridge: Polity Press.

Guttmann, A. (1978) *From Ritual to Record.* New York: Columbia University Press.

Hague, E. and Mercer, J. (1998) 'Geographical memory and urban identity in Scotland: Raith Rovers FC and Kirkaldy', *Geography*, 83, 2, pp. 105-16.

Inglis, S. (1983) *The Football Grounds of England and Wales.* London: Collins.

Inglis, S. (2000) *Sightlines: A stadium odyssey.* London: Yellow Jersey Press.

Lenskyj, H.J. (1998) 'Sport and corporate environmentalism: the case of the Sydney 2000 Olympics', *International Review for the Sociology of Sport*, 33, 4, pp. 341-54.

Maguire, J. (1999) *Global Sport: Identities, societies, civilizations.* Cambridge: Polity Press.

Pryce, R. (1989) *Scotland's Golf Courses.* Aberdeen: University of Aberdeen Press.

Waylen, P. and Snook, A. (1990) 'Patterns of regional success in the Football League, 1921-1988', *Area*, 22, 4, pp. 353-67.